How to Master the Art of
Hand-to-Hand Sales

Dave Thomas

Table of Contents

How to Master the Art of
Hand-to-Hand Sales

Dave Thomas

Introduction

Since the days of bartering and trade, the ability to sell has been essential in conducting hand-to-hand business in the world. In those days, even though there was no exchange of money, you still had to show that your merchandise was worth trading for. Then, as money came into the picture, you had to prove that your product was worth buying. Those sellers who were charismatic, clever, well-spoken, persuasive, and persistent always did well in the early days of bartering, trade, and business in the marketplace. These same characteristics continued to bring success to sellers all over the world throughout history, and still applies to those who are, and seek to be, successful in sales today.

As a child, I always wanted things from adults and other children, but I had to figure out a way to get it. I soon learned that in order to get what you want you had to present a good reason for somebody to give it to you. In life we are constantly marketing and selling ourselves to potential friends, romantic interests, employers, and business partners. The art of sales is something we use in many areas of our life without realizing it. I have done many jobs that involved some aspect of marketing, promotion, and sales in my life, and I have learned many things along the way. From the art of upselling at my first job at McDonald's to eventually starting a Seamoss Drink Company selling hand-to-hand on the street, at work, at pop-ups and expos, and eventually wholesale to stores and restaurants.

My mother and grandmother often told me stories of how they sold handmade clothes and food in the marketplace in Jamaica to survive when times were hard. They brought that same survival mentality with them when they came to America, and that mentality always stuck with them, even though they got better jobs in finance and healthcare in this country.

I worked as a door-to-door salesman for wholesale companies at 18-years-old. I hustled and sold cigarettes and other things on the streets of New York City to survive during hard times. Initially I was awkward and shy, especially as a door-to-door salesman, but the need for money and that survival instinct motivated me to learn and improve as a salesperson.

In this book, I hope to share what I have learned in my journey as an ambitious but inexperienced child to becoming a very successful hand-to-hand salesman, so that you too can become a great salesperson and reap the rewards of my proven hand-to-hand sale strategies.

1

The Four Ps of Sales

The 4 Ps of Sales

Product
Pricing
Presence
Pitch

1. Know your PRODUCT

Know your product inside and out so you can highlight the benefits to your potential customer and answer their questions accurately.

2. PRICE accordingly and leave room for a sale or a bargain

It's common for big and small businesses to overprice or mark up a product in order to then mark down the product or offer a sale to give the customer the feeling of getting a deal or a bargain.

3. Have a good PRESENCE

Establish a good connection with the potential customer and try to make them comfortable with you in a smooth and effortless way. Try to use humor to break through any early resistance to your pitch. Be respectful and never touch them or invade their personal space. Use any information you can gain from their appearance, response, or actions to make a connection and establish a dialogue with them. Try to be straightforward and direct so you waste as little time as possible. Don't be awkward or show signs of nervousness; just be yourself and use your personality to develop your own personal style of selling that works for you. Don't tell them the price; let them ask for it themselves because that shows their level of interest and intent to purchase if the price is favorable to them.

4. Know your PITCH in and out and keep it short

Time is money and if you take up too much of people's time you probably won't get their money.

$$P - O = Pr$$

Price minus Overhead equals Profit

2

Know your Strengths and Weaknesses

Know your strengths and maximize them. What are you naturally good at? Are you a funny person? Do you have a good memory? Are you charismatic? Do you have a great smile? Do you have a great sense of style? Are you an attractive person? Are you good at engaging in conversation? At some point you should analyze yourself and think about what you're naturally good at and try to think about how you can improve and incorporate them into your sales strategy and approach.

On the opposite end of the spectrum, you must also identify your weaknesses and slowly improve in those areas. We all struggle (or have struggled) in certain areas when attempting to make a hand-to-hand sale. Some of us lack confidence and get nervous when we have to talk to potential customers and make our pitch. Some of us don't smile or seem very friendly and inviting. Some of us have a bad memory and forget important information about our product. Some of us lack enthusiasm and excitement when engaging potential customers. Whatever your weakness is, you should figure it out and actively start working to improve so you can be a better salesperson.

Finally, create an effective selling style that works with your unique personality. Some people have dynamic personalities, and some have more calm or quiet personalities. There are many different types of people in the world, but a lot of people believe you have to be super animated and very outgoing to be a good salesperson. However, the reality is this is not true. You just have to get the potential customer's attention and create a connection with them and pique their interest in your product. I have traveled all over to pop-up shops and expos, and I have met vendors with all kinds of personalities. I have met quiet vendors who listen closely to your questions and give you precise information on their product that piques your interest in making a purchase. I have also met loud vendors with a great sense of humor that make potential customers laugh and feel entertained while making a sale. I have met vendors who were very serious about their product and had very well put together demonstrations to show potential customers that captivated their attention. I have also met a lot of vendors who were very laid back and smooth with customers, making them feel very comfortable during the sales experience. The most important thing is to know your personality and use what makes you special and unique to make a connection with potential customers.

3
Create the Perfect Atmosphere for Spending

When we walk into a mall, a department store, or even our local supermarket, there are things that are arranged in order to influence you to spend more money. The music playing, the color paint used, the aroma, the lights, the sale markers, etc. Billions of dollars are spent every year on extensive research in advertising, marketing, and psychology to accomplish this.

In the world of hand-to-hand sales, this is also very important but in a slightly different way. For us salespeople, we have to create an atmosphere for spending by how we greet people and how we make them feel around us while trying to make a sale. Whether it's one-on-one or you're selling to a group of people, you have to create some level of buzz and interest in what you're selling in order to catch and keep their attention long enough to make them want to buy what you're selling. You can play music, you can use samples, your initial greeting, your display, asking certain questions that allow people to open up and feel comfortable talking to you, or even something you're wearing that catches people's attention and causes them to start a conversation with you. Whatever you use, it must be well thought out, tested, and eventually become a proven idea that creates an atmosphere for spending everywhere you go.

4
Developing Relationships with Your Customers

Developing relationships with your customers is the key to getting repeat customers for life. In a world that is addicted to social media, we have become less social with each other. As a result, we crave real connections more than ever. The better the relationships we form with our customers, the more loyal they will be to your business. As consumers, we all are loyal to the brands we love and the salespeople that make us feel good.

The best way to build solid relationships with your customers is to be pleasant and genuinely be concerned about what matters to them. Asking how they are doing, how they are feeling, what they do, where they are from, what their interests are, trying to find things that you and that person have in common, and being completely genuine in your interaction with them will help them connect with you and make them feel comfortable. This will make them have more positive feelings towards you and they will be more likely to make a purchase from you. Also, after that purchase they will want to do business with you again because of the positive connection they made with you.

5
Plant The Seeds of Sales

We have all tried to make a sale with a potential customer and then they declined for whatever reason. Well, all hope is not lost because you can always sow the seeds of future sales with that customer, or even a group of potential customers, who may not make a purchase the first time around.

There are several reasons why people choose not to buy something from even the best salespeople and you have to learn quickly to find out the reason and cleverly turn it into a reason for them to buy something next time.

Let's say they say, "I can't afford it right now." You can easily respond and say something like, "That's such a shame. This is such a great product I would hate for you to miss out on it, but I'll be back another day. Maybe if you have the money, you can buy it next time."

Many times, a potential customer will say they may buy something next time and some will even PROMISE to buy something next time! The promise is what you really want to hear because most people are inclined to want to keep a promise if they make one. This is a seed of sales that you want to plant by putting the idea of them buying next time in the mind of your potential customer, hoping that they water that seed by considering or agreeing to a future purchase. The more likeable and entertaining you are, the more likely they will respond in a positive way.

If they say they don't need it, then you must show them how they need it – or even better, show them why they should want it. You have to learn the art of being suggestive and persuasive when trying to get someone to consider a future purchase. If one of your regular customers, or someone who has bought something before, happens to be nearby use them as a testimonial on how great your product is. People are always more inclined to buy something after hearing exciting and convincing five-star reviews, especially if it comes from one of their peers.

Every time you talk up your product and advertise how wonderful it is, you sow seeds of curiosity in the person's mind. Make sure to always introduce and describe your product in such a way that everyone who doesn't buy definitely remembers it in a way that will make them more inclined to want to purchase it in the future, or even change their mind in a few minutes. If you have a sample, that can also be a seed of potential future sales.

6
Choose Your Words Wisely

To be a great salesperson, you have to be strategic with your words. A big part of advertising and marketing are words, and the people who write these words are paid very well. In the same way, if you use the right words when making your pitch to a potential customer, it will pay off for you too in increased sales.

People love to spend money on things they want and think they need. So, you must always introduce your product with the elements of want and necessity. For example: If you have a beverage, you can advertise it as "Healthy and Delicious." Most people would buy it for either reason, but they would want to buy it even more when both elements are present. You also want to describe your product as offering value, convenience, and as a bargain. Some customers are impulsive spenders, and some are critical thinking shoppers who are looking and listening carefully to hear how they really benefit from buying what you're selling. Try not to talk too much about yourself. A brief introduction is good, and then get straight into your main pitch.

Practice the art of the "soft sell," where you can persuade someone into making a purchase without them feeling any pressure at all. Be suggestive in your selling pitch. Similar to seduction, pleasant persuasion often makes a purchase even more enjoyable to a person. Use words that are very descriptive and appealing to the ears that create intrigue and desire in the minds of potential customers.

7
Recognizing and Taking Advantage of a Selling Opportunity

With costs of living continuing to rise faster than the average income, more and more people are starting small businesses to meet their financial obligations. They offer their products or services at pop-up shops, flea markets, expos, and any other venues they can find. Sometimes there is an opportunity to sell your product right in front of you, but you can't recognize it or you're afraid to make the approach because of fear of rejection. The key is to be always looking out and listening for opportunities. Then when you find them, you must inquire about it, plan your approach, and then execute it. You must maintain a positive, optimistic (but realistic) attitude.

In order to accomplish anything in life you must be willing to try. If you never try, then you have already failed, and if at first you don't succeed, try again. Sometimes it may not work out, but you have to continue to seek out opportunities to sell your products with family, friends, co-workers, strangers, and other businesses. There might be a Farmer's Market in your neighborhood you don't know about where you can sell your product or a store owner willing to put your product on their shelves. The only way to find out is to go ask questions and introduce them to your product. That person may not be interested but they can refer you to someone who is interested. You never know what one interaction can lead to. A lot of my success has come by way of third parties.

Another important skill to develop is recognizing when collaborating with other business owners could potentially be mutually beneficial to your business. Sometimes two businesses complement each other perfectly, and it makes sense to partner together to reach more customers. Always have an open mind and be willing to think outside the box and try new things to improve your sales and marketing. Also, if you have an idea that might help someone else's business, tell them because by genuinely helping them, they will be more inclined to want to help you be successful too.

Lastly, don't be afraid to travel or go outside your comfort zone to make sales or expand into a different market. Many businesses have grown substantially because the owner decided to travel to a different city or state and see how their business does in a different place with different people. Sometimes you have exactly what a lot of people want but you're in the wrong place. Location can definitely be the difference maker and a game changer in your business.

8
Don't Give Up or Get Distracted

Any business or job that requires you to make sales is going to have its ups and downs. It can be very stressful and even depressing when you don't make any sales. You may start doubting your sales skills, your product, or even your entire business altogether. In these moments it's important to remember everyone makes mistakes and has off days when they may not bring their A-game, or even get zero sales despite doing an excellent job pitching their product. Nobody's perfect, and even the best salesperson in the world has bad days.

A good salesperson is persistent, stays optimistic, and maintains a pleasant demeanor despite the result. You have to be confident in your product and your pitch and keep going no matter what to ultimately achieve success.

Sometimes you will encounter negative people who may even try to discourage others from supporting your business and you have to know how to deal with them in a pleasant, clever, and professional way so they don't negatively influence potential customers that are around. You must remain focused on your goals, believing in yourself and your product at all times. If you don't, then you will want to give up when you have bad days or when things are going wrong.

Surround yourself with people who are positive and uplifting people who are successful and who will encourage you to keep going when times get tough. People with experience who have been where you are and didn't give up and are now successful. These types of people will be your greatest source of inspiration and motivation. Read or listen to the life stories of great entrepreneurs and salespeople in history, and go to motivational seminars to get recharged and refocused when you feel that spark dying down.

All these things will help you to keep going and become the great salesperson and entrepreneur I know you are. If you believe in yourself then I believe in you! Go out there and be the great salesperson I know you can be!

If this book has helped you in any way, please recommend it to someone else so they too can become a great salesperson. Resources like this can really be a great help to someone who is just starting out in sales or even a seasoned salesperson who needs some inspiration to keep going when times get tough.

Bonus Tips: Learn to master the art of the up-sale and always recommend your products to your potential customers as gifts for their family and friends, especially if they say they're not interested or it's not something they could use.